AF454412

THE SIXTH SENSE

ITS CULTIVATION AND USE

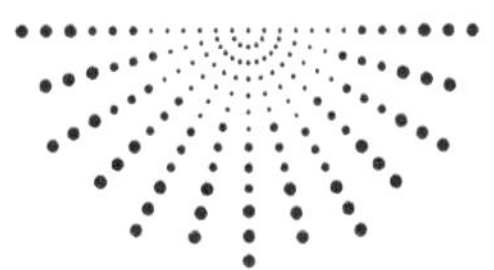

CHARLES HENRY BRENT

ALICIA EDITIONS

" The only real valuable thing is intuition."

— ALBERT EINSTEIN

CONTENTS

INTRODUCTORY NOTE

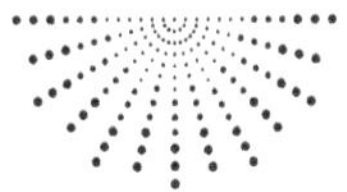

This book was planned and promised to the publisher more than three years ago. Exacting duties have compelled the writer from time to time, to defer the completion of his undertaking. The delay has been profitable in that it has afforded opportunity for the study of recent works on kindred topics, which in some respects has modified and in some enlarged the original conception of the subject in hand. A long ocean voyage at last has provided the quiet in which to write out these thoughts.

SS. Prinz Eitel Friedrich.

CHAPTER 1. THE SIXTH SENSE

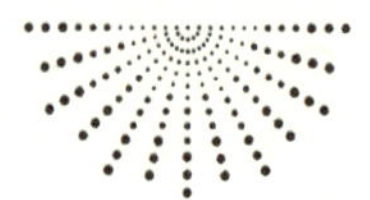

By the Sixth Sense I mean the Mystic Sense, or that inner perceptive faculty which distinguishes man from the highest below him and allies him to the highest above him. So distinctive among created objects is it of man that it might, not inaptly, be characterized as the Human Sense. It is used for no one exclusive purpose; on the contrary it is only under its operation that man's activities, one and all, become human. In its nature it differs essentially from the bodily senses though we are justified in thinking of it as a sense because its function is, like them, to perceive and to afford food for thought.

The five bodily senses originally, in the first stages of evolution, were, and, in their ultimate aspect are, one sense—the sense of touch. By means of it plant, mollusc and worm relate themselves to the universe of which they are a part. By degrees the single sense, in the evolutionary process, finds opportunity and occasion for specialization. Sight is extraordinarily sensitized touch by means of which form and color are perceived, and the distant object comes bowing to our feet; the stars, leaping across space, are converted into intimate friends, and earth's farthest horizon lies at our door. Hearing is touch localized and specialized so as to be capable of perceiving the vibrations caused by the impact of one body upon another; its enlarged capacity classifies sound in such a way as to offer its mutations and subtleties for our use and pleasure as the weaver offers his threads to the loom. Smell is that specialization of touch, uniquely delicate, supposed by Maeterlinck to be still in its earlier stage of development in human kind, which responds to the stimulus of those otherwise intangible exhalations called odor. Lastly, taste is touch specialized so as to discern the inner properties of food stuff; taste is the testing sense. Mere touch determines the existence, specialized touch the character and niceties of matter of the physical universe.

As indicative of the unity of the animal senses and the cooperative sympathy between them, it is noteworthy that when one sense is impaired or destroyed, the others diligently endeavor to supply its absence, the entire body playing the part as far as possible of eye or ear or both, and each remaining sense growing extraordinarily acute so as to take on somewhat of the character of the most nearly affiliated or the neighbor sense. The blind man can almost see with ears and hands, the deaf can almost hear with eyes. The senses that are left strain, not without a measure of success, to convey to the brain impressions for which they are not congenitally adapted.

The organic differences in the bodily senses, then, find a close unity in functional similarity, all the sensory nerves grouping themselves under the head of touch. The Mystic Sense, likewise, first comes to our attention as a simple faculty of perception by which we gain cognition of that department of reality that transcends bodily touch and its sub-divisions, but study reveals that its unity is ordered complexity, as in the case of all developed endowments. Broadly speaking it is the sense which relates man to the spiritual or psychic aspect of reality. It puts us into relation with the spiritual order of which we are a part. It finds room for exercise, gains its freedom, and reaches its highest development in this sphere, beginning operations at the point where the bodily senses are compelled by inherent limitations to halt. It discerns the innermost character, use, value of the objective, and differentiates between the human and the animal estimate of things. Indeed it has in it that which is not of this world or order. It soars beyond human and mundane affairs and steeps its wings in Divine altitudes where the throne of God is set. Not only does it perceive but it also lays hold of and appropriates that phase of reality which lies beyond the unaided reach, or eludes the grasp, of all the rest of our faculties in their happiest combination, and therefore of any one of them independently. It takes the material gathered by physical contact with the world of sight and sound, and presents it to the mind for rationalizing operations. More than that, it comes back freighted with wealth gathered in explorations in regions where neither body nor reason can tread, converting life's dull prose into poetry and song.

The most alert and indispensable of endowments, it is at once sociable with the remainder of man's faculties, external and internal, and jealously independent of them saving of human consciousness alone. In its higher stages of development it accepts suggestions from all, dictation from none. Its manner is courteous and its mode of approach one of promptings and hints. The sphere of every other faculty is its sphere where it is content to play the modest part of a handmaiden, never usurping functions already provided for, although it has a sphere of its own whither not even reason can follow. It is supplementary to all, contradictory to none. Without its exercise there can be no progress or growth. It has its origin in a groping instinct, its final development in orderly activities capable of increasingly clear classification. Body, intellect, character, moral and religious, are under its influence and dependent upon its beneficent operations. It plays upon the body, contributing to its health and efficiency; it gives wings to the intellect, making it creative and productive, capable of formulating hypotheses and venturing upon speculation; it converts the seemingly impossible into the normal, bringing moral ideals within reach of the will, without which improvement in character would be a matter of chance; it unfolds the Divine to the human and forms a nexus between here and beyond, now and to-morrow, finite and infinite, God and man. It looks not only up but down, making the nature outside of us intelligible to the nature inside of us and friendly with it. If it peoples the stars, it also makes a universe of the atom. It is mysterious, recollective, emotional, intuitive, speculative, imaginative, prophetic, minatory, expectant, penetrative. As it moves up or down with equal freedom, so it reaches backward or forward, is attached or detached at will, in its operations.

The Sixth Sense, or, to be more accurate, the second group of senses, has its specialized functions, difficult as it is to analyze with accuracy this most spiritual endowment of human personality, the inner gift of touch. It has specializations parallel to those of the bodily senses. Sight, hearing and testing are its functions. So clear eyed is it that it can see with the nicety of an eye aided by the microscope, so sensitive to voices that the lowest whispers impart a message, so critical as to test values with a precision and swiftness that surpass the taste and smell which tell us what is sweet and what unsavory.

If it be argued that I am but dilating on certain aspects of mind, I am not concerned to deny that all may be comprehended under that convenient blanket-word. But they are as distinct from the rationalizing media as from the will.

The nearest approach to a satisfactory substitute for the term "mystic sense" in terms of the reason is "conceptual reason." It furnishes us with the thought of a faculty which has procreative or generative properties capable of being fertilized by intercourse with that which is separate from and higher than itself. Its first activity is to lay itself over against that which, though partaking of its own nature, is not itself. It is not self-fertilizing and can conceive or beget only after having perceived and apprehended.[1] It has constant regard for an objective and communication with it.

The operation of the Mystic Sense is summed up in the single word faith, which is described as the giving substance to that which is hoped for, the testing of things not seen.[2] There is no objection to letting the world faith cover the whole working of the Mystic Sense, provided it is not restricted to a severely religious meaning. It is thus that it is commonly understood, or at any rate when applied in other connections it is assumed to be the working of a different faculty from that exercised in the sphere of religion. In its distinctively religious meaning, faith is the operation of the Mystic Sense in its highest employment. There is no one faculty that is reserved exclusively for religious employment. The fact is that religious faith is no more separate from the processes of the Mystic Sense which appropriate health for the body, hypotheses for the mind, working principles for the man of action, and ideals for the character, or independent of them, than the act of physical perception, which enables us to touch the stars, is separate from that use of the sensory nerves which relates us to the book we handle, or independent of it. They are both the result of a single faculty, or group of faculties, operating in different altitudes. Faith will be accepted in these pages as a philosophic term. Thus we speak of scientific faith, moral faith, and religious faith with equal appropriateness, meaning the Mystic Sense operating respectively in the interests of the scientific, of the moral, and of the religious.

The Mystic Sense has for its workshop the uplands of life in the rarefied atmosphere of ideas and ideals. It is at once a super-sense giving us a bird's-eye view of the universe which is not permitted at close quarters, and a sub-sense bringing before our attention the contents hidden beneath the surface of things. There are not two worlds, objective and subjective respectively, but two aspects of one world— things as they are in their absolute and ultimate being, and things as they are relatively or as apprehended by our cognitive powers. Our conception of the truth is a distortion or falls short of the truth, and it is our aspiration to bring about such a coincidence as will make the relation of subject to object perfect. We draw the thing as we see it for the God of things as they are now, not to-morrow only, the sole difference being that to-morrow our painting will be truer to the original and consequently more artistic than now. All objective is immediately reduced by man, by subconscious or conscious process, into subjective, so that we may for the sake of convenience talk of subjective and objective phases of reality, the subjective being human, partial, progressive, the objective being divine, absolute, and final.

There is an objective physical world and an objective psychic or spiritual world, the latter being immanent in the former, though not limited by it, so that every material object has spiritual contents. The spiritual is no more an inside without an outside than the physical is an outside without an inside. Each has its phase of reality, though in the ultimate analysis the physical is dependent for its value upon its spiritual capacity. The physical has a non-sensible inside which to be discerned calls for distinctively human as distinguished from mere animal powers of perception. Dimly in animal life there is a recognition of inner character in objects— hostility, affinity, nourishment and the like are instinctively sensed; but here deep perception stops except where, by reason of what is called domestication or association with man, certain human characteristics are faintly imaged in dog or horse.

There is no antagonism between the physical and the spiritual. The physical world is to man a medium through which phases of the spiritual are reached. The only antagonism there can be is that which arises by an attempt to use the material without regard for its full spiritual contents or inside. Were not the physical universe a sacrament it would be a phantasm. If man divorces the inside from the outside with a view to gratifying his physical senses he abdicates his character as a man to become an animal; if to feed anything less than his entire selfhood, he presents the spectacle of arrested development. The bodily senses alone can get at the full content, the deep inside of nothing, no matter how pronounced its objectivity, "The truly real is a thing that has an inside."[3] The more pronounced or attractive the external substance and form of a material object and the closer we are to it, the greater the difficulty for the average character to gain cognition of its spiritual essence. "How hardly shall they that have riches enter into the Kingdom of God."[4] Even those who place an undue valuation upon the material, whether possessed of wealth or not, have a like difficulty in penetrating into the internal realm which lies beneath and around as well as above and within the external.[5] It is absurd for men to expect to sense the spiritual except with spiritual faculties. The physical world is perceived by a sensory apparatus of the same substance as that of the physical world; the spiritual world is perceived by a sensory apparatus of the same substance as that of the spiritual world. There must be an inherent affinity between the thing apprehended and the organ apprehending. Now the natural man receiveth not the things of the Spirit of God; for they are foolishness unto him; and he cannot know them because they are spiritually proved.[6]

Reality is a term too often confined to that which can be expressed in terms of bodily senses; whereas it is that which has existence in heaven above, in the earth beneath, and in the waters under the earth, and which, apart from human perception, though in a minimum degree or passively, plays upon and affects man and his universe, but which reaches its highest potentiality manward when, by the volitional operation of human faculties it is subjectively apprehended and finds permanent place in his consciousness. Reality is that which supports and feeds the subconscious life by the pressure of its mere existence or laws of being, but which is capable of bestowing larger gifts in proportion to the degree in which it receives conscious admission into the activities of personal experience. It is a law of spiritual or psychic, as well as of physical, existence that every part is related to every other part and influenced by it through either attraction or energy. In the case of inanimate matter mere spacial propinquity or distance determines the measure of attraction or energy of object upon object, but where sentient beings are concerned the reaction of conscious volition on environment is the determining factor regulating the degree of influence released.

The search for the real in internal processes cannot ignore the external. Conversely the activities of the workaday world cannot summarily dismiss the internal.[7] The physical senses have a modest but indispensable part to play under the primacy of the Mystic Sense. The normal use of the Mystic Sense does not make a mystic. The healthily developed man is mystical though not a mystic. His dominating sense is that of the spirit, not that of the flesh. A mystic, technically defined, is a specialist in the subjective or internal, just as a collector is a specialist in the objective or external. There is no danger in either extreme except so far as its votary adopts an exclusive attitude toward its seeming opposite (which really is its complement), or toward the balance of human thought and life. A deliberate and persistent use of the Mystic Sense without respect for the objective would be subversive of all progress and a reversion to chaos. "The progress of thought consists in gradually separating the series of objective and universally valid, from that of subjective experiences. In the measure that their confusion prevails, man is, to all intents and purposes, mad; and it is this note of insanity that characterizes medicine and religion in their early stages. Dreams and reality are mixed up; subjective connections are objectified."[8] If the objective and the subjective may not be divorced and set at odds against one another, neither may they be confused. Both errors would result in disorder and hopeless perplexity.

The serious crux is how, in the realm of the spiritual and the physically intangible, to distinguish between the real and the seeming, the true and the false. This it is the function of the Mystic Sense to do aided by the full complement of inner faculties. In a measure the Mystic Sense, like the bodily senses, acts automatically, but like them it needs special training in order to separate phantasm from reality, to determine values, and to grade and classify ideals until they reveal themselves to be ordered unity, not less but more mysterious because more intelligible or apprehensible by the whole man. The first principle to lay down is that no man can treat himself as a unit or credit the findings of his Mystic Sense with absolute or final authority until he has tried them by some valid corporate test. Neither sight, nor hearing, nor touch, used without regard to the experience of others and respect for it, can fail to lead us astray. The conclusions of the wisest and the competent register themselves from age to age, coming to us in the shape of beneficent authority to prevent a man from repeating work that has already been done and well done. Verification is not contemptuous of authority, though he flouts authority, indeed, who ignores it in a process of individualistic experiments. Pure individualism at best can apprehend but a fragment of reality and at worst declines into eccentricity or even insanity. Those who are really educated recognize their relation to a social whole and bring the results of their sense perceptions, before accepting their verdict, to be tested by the age-long, man-wide experiences of humanity as formulated in the accepted conclusions of their generation and found in its institutions and customs. Universal experience is never wholly but only approximately infallible, yet accurate enough to be authoritative for corrective purposes. By respectful attention to it, individual judgment is checked in possible error and at the same time is given opportunity to offer its own contribution to the totality of knowledge, a contribution which may endorse, modify, or enlarge that already reached. In this way only is society preserved from becoming a mob of eccentrics and fanatics, each whirling in his own little circle. Commerce, art, science, letters, government, religion—in short every department of life you can think of requires such a mode of procedure for the protection of reality in its varied manifestations and for the protection of the individual against himself. But in no conditions is a social checking off of findings more essential than in the psychic or spiritual realm. Mystical experience organizes itself or is consciously organized in a sufficient degree to give men that high kind of freedom which comes to us when we act with constant reference to the fact that we are members one of another, so that the experience of the human race is ours wherewith to enrich ourselves. A mystic of the type of St. Theresa, who could hardly see the objective in her rush past form to reach idea, could not be distinguished from the inmate of a madhouse who insists that his tinsel crown is the diadem of a Napoleon, unless she interpreted her personal experience in relation to the spiritual consciousness of Christendom. "Once," writes this saint, "when I was holding in my hand the cross of my rosary, He took it from me into His own hand. He returned it; but it was then four large stones incomparably more precious than diamonds: the five wounds were delineated on them with the most admirable art. He said to me that for the future that cross would appear so to me always, and so it did. The precious stones were seen, however, only by myself."[9] A madman would have omitted the last sentence. Her mystical experience was individual though it preserved for its foundation a background of universal experience. It united her to her fellows, instead of separating her from them.

The law of use is as applicable to the Mystic Sense as to the rest of the gifts and endowments which make up the completeness of human personality. Its exercise enlarges its capacity and quickens its general efficiency; if used through the whole range of its opportunities, it becomes a hardy faculty, trustworthy in every sphere where its responsibility lies; specialization of operation in one direction, to the partial neglect of other departments open to it, produces acuteness in one direction and dulness in other directions which is characteristic of specialists in science; if the specialization is so exclusive as to shut off observation and consideration of every interest but one, there must ensue lopsided growth and maimed personality.

It is the purpose of this book to trace the operation of the Mystic Sense in normal manhood through the major departments of human experience in order to encourage greater confidence in this wonderful gift, to appeal for a more comprehensive use of it, and to indicate how it may be cultivated.

NOTE TO CHAPTER 1.

Von Hügel in his study of the Mystical Element of Religion concludes that there is "no distinct faculty of mystical apprehension." In a passage following this contention (vol. II, pp. 283, 284), he so states his position as to make it possible for me to start from a contradictory assertion and reach his conclusion. We agree that mysticism is "not everything in any one soul, but something in every soul of man."

The entire passage reads as follows:

"Is there, then, strictly speaking, such a thing as a specifically distinct, self-sufficing, purely Mystical mode of apprehending Reality? I take it, distinctly not; and that all the errors of the Exclusive Mystic proceed precisely from the contention that Mysticism does constitute such an entirely separate, completely self-supported kind of human experience. This denial does not, of course, mean that soul does not differ quite indefinitely from soul, in the amount and kind of the recollective, intuitive, deeply emotive element possessed and exercised by it concurrently or alternately with other elements, —the sense of the Infinite within and without the Finite springing up in the soul on occasion of its contact with the Contingent; nor, again, that these more or less congenital differences and vocations amongst souls cannot be and are not still further developed by grace and heroism into types of religious apprehension and life, so strikingly divergent, as, at first sight, to seem hardly even supplementary the one to the other. But it means that, in even the most purely contingent-seeming soul, and in its apparently but Institutional and Historical assents and acts, there ever is, there can never fail to be, some, however, implicit, however slight, however intermittent, sense and experience of the Infinite, evidenced by at least some dissatisfaction with the Finite, except as this Finitude is an occasion for growth in, and a part-expression of, that Infinite, our true home. And, again, it means, that even the most exclusively mystical-seeming soul ever depends, for the fulness and healthiness of even the most purely mystical of its acts and states, as really upon its past and present contacts with the Contingent, Temporal, and Spacial, and with social facts and elements, as upon its movement of concentration, and the sense and experience, evoked on occasion of those contacts or of their memories, of the Infinite within and around those finitudes and itself.

"Only thus does Mysticism attain to its true, full dignity, which consists precisely in being, not everything in any one soul, but something in every soul of man; and in presenting at its fullest, the amplest development, among certain special natures with the help of certain special graces and heroisms, or what, in some degree, and form, is present in every truly human soul, and in such a soul's every, at all genuine and complete, grace-stimulated religious act and state. And only thus does it, as Partial Mysticism, retain all the strength and escape the weaknesses and dangers of would-be Pure Mysticism, as regards the mode and character or Religious Experience, Knowledge, and Life."

If my interpretation of this writer be correct, he terms that a "recollective, intuitive, deeply emotive element" which I conceive to be a mystic faculty or sense. The fact that it pervades every part of human personality does not disqualify it from claiming the dignity of a distinctive faculty. It bears a similar relation to the higher endowments of personality which the ether bears to light and to the call of world to world. The Mystic Sense is the enabling faculty, which makes man human. Its pervasiveness does not detract from, rather does it enhance, its distinctness. To call it an element seems to clothe it in a vagueness which its character does not merit. If man were merely a phase of matter, we could employ the term element with propriety. That which can be only an element in a universe, at any rate may be a faculty or sense in man.

---

1. It is only partially true to say that concept follows upon percept. Their action is simultaneous more nearly than consecutive. Conceptualism as a complete system cannot perhaps stand but in its origin it was a healthy reaction against both nominalism and realism, as well as a mediator combining the good in both.
2. Heb. XI:1.
3. Von Hügel, The Mystical Element of Religion, vol. II, p. 264.
4. Mk. X:23.
5. Mk. X:24, 25.
6. Ψυχικὸς δὲ ἄνθρωπος οὐ δέχεται τὰ τοῦ Πνεύματος τοῦ Θεοῦ; μωρία γὰρ αὐτῷ ἐστι, καὶ οὐ δύναται γνῶναι, ὅτι πνευματικῶς ἀνακρίνεται. 1 Cor. II, 14.
7. "True priority and superiority lies, not with one of these constituents against the other, but with the total subjective

—objective interaction or resultant, which is superior, and indeed gives their place and worth to, those interdependent parts."—Von Hügel's Mystical Element of Religion, vol. II, p. 114.
8. Tyrrell's Christianity at the Cross Roads, p. 240.
9. Quoted by Von Hügel, vol. II, p. 18.

CHAPTER 2. IN RELATION TO HEALTH

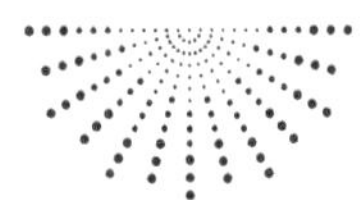

There is nothing so multiple in its composition, and yet nothing so seemingly simple, so unit-like a unity, as normal personality— a normal character englobed by a normal body. Normality is the product of a two-fold force, the true interrelation between the organs of the body and a similar interrelation between the inner faculties, culminating in a rhythmic interaction between the two. The normal man acts in the completeness of his manhood in all that he does, never adopting the rôle of either mere machine or mere ghost. In so far as the inside and the outside of man work as a unity, the dignity of human personality manifests itself; any departure from harmony approaches that dangerous borderland beyond which lies disintegration and disorder. Disease is a lack of rhythm, a note in the scale out of tune. Health is harmony.

Up to the time that consciousness of existence awakens, the processes of life operate under the stimulus and protection of the human and physical environment which surround the infant. With the immediate effect of suitable shelter and wholesome nourishment we are fairly conversant. As to just what direct or indirect influence psychic surroundings have upon the subconscious life of a baby, we are not in a position to dogmatize, though we can arrive inferentially at certain rational probabilities.

Apparently the infant, and certainly the child, is extraordinarily sensitive to subtle forces. Acting upon this supposition the Christian Church from the beginning, by a symbolic and sacramental act, has aimed to thrust children deep into the bosom of God by the rite of baptism, and claimed for them not only a place but a place of chief importance in the spiritual society. Instinctively the mother, with exquisite solicitude, whispers her ideals for the future of her offspring into the ears of the babe at her breast, talking as though to one whose consciousness were awake. In this way Samuels have been raised to Israel. At the close of each day the mother bids her child sleep by singing lullabies and hanging mystic poppies over wide-awake eyes. She speaks in the highest type of language, in poetry adorned with song, to this little unconscious scrap of humanity. In other words her mystic sense is pressing upon the mystic sense of her child as naturally and fittingly as her arms fold the infant body and her lips touch its cheek.

Unless positive proof to the contrary is adduced, it is safe to believe that it makes a great difference to the child's after life of what sort its psychic environment is during its first years on earth, whether the minds about it are healthy, expressing themselves healthily, whether the tone of family life is hopeful and spiritual. Though it cannot finally determine the course that the child's life will take, at any rate it affords the best opportunity for making it a worthy course. My conviction is, that the difference between good and bad psychic environment for a baby is the same as that between healthy and unhealthy vegetable environment for a young plant. An infant abandoned by its mother to the care of nurses and servants, be the provision for its animal comfort and safety what it may, begins life with a minimum of opportunity. Man is not born mere animal but man from the first breath. Therefore from the first breath he needs man's surroundings. In order that his latent character may have its best chance, he ought to be given the most congenial human environment available. If there is no conscious self, at any rate there is a subconscious self, struggling at a very early moment by baby smiles and frets, gropings and babblings to utter itself. Psychology seems to have reached at least this conclusion—that the subconscious is, that it is the fundamental part of man, that it is his most sensitive self, never relinquishing that which it grasps and grasping everything that touches it.

Psychic forces may influence mightily the subconscious life of an infant and promote healthy character, but have they any effect on physical well-being? The reply would seem to be that, if at any time in the span of a lifetime they work beneficently in this direction, it is probable that they do so from the outset. It would be sheer waste of time to adduce arguments to prove that healthy minds conduce directly to healthy physique. The difficulty is to find the limit of such influence, so vast is it. Physical well-being, however, is not an end in itself, and it is a subversion of the human order to aim at health of mind or character in order that our physique may be improved. So nicely is human nature proportioned and adjusted that it is doubtful whether a person could achieve physical health by becoming good with that sole end in view. Physical health is not essential to a high degree of human efficiency, though health of character is and therefore must be sought first because of its priceless value. But it is our just assumption that a child with a healthy body is more likely to have a normal inner personality than if it had a sickly body. Outer and inner health act and react and interact so that it is equally true to say that, given a healthy mind and disposition, other things being equal, the body will have the best opportunity of being normal and, whatever its condition, of being used to the best advantage. There can be no consideration of higher importance than to make a child sensitive as soon after birth as possible, to his psychic, moral, and mystical environment. It will conduce to loftiness of character and, for aught we know, to useful longevity and vigor of physique.

Only soulless animals can be satisfied with physical splendor or count muscle sufficient in itself. Man by virtue of his manhood can never live according to merely animal laws. His animal nature itself is ultimately weakened if he does. In proportion as he has fine physique he must develop a fine mind and character. If not, unrestrained passion and ruin stare him in the face. The body finds its full meaning and so its possibilities, only when the soul has discovered itself and claimed its liberty. It is then alone that a whole army of anxieties and fears is scattered, leaving the body free and joyously adventurous, ready to identify its movements with those of the soul. Consequently it is not illogical or untrue to say that the first requisite for physical efficiency of a child is to insure that whatever its subconscious life is able to drink in should be sweet, wholesome, and strong. The tone of domestic life, the character of the child's attendants, the whole expanse of human bosom on which it lies and from which it receives nourishment, ought to be as near what one would wish it to be if from the first the little babe had a conscious as well as a subconscious self, and were a morally responsible and not a mere non-moral agent. There can be a healthy domestic environment for the keen-eyed, deep-seeing child only when it has been preceded by a similar environment for the baby. What the tone was for the purely subconscious, it will be for the conscious life when it awakes. Therefore even though parents are skeptical of their influence upon infant subconsciousness, they cannot dispense with attention to its character if they hope to bring beneficial pressure to bear on the child's conscious life. From the first they must learn to deal with a baby as a moral being, impressionable beyond observation.

When we turn to man's conscious life and the relation between health of body and a healthy consciousness we are on more demonstrable ground. Experience has proved that our external and internal faculties work in sympathy with one another. If the body is distressed, the inner consciousness droops; if the inner consciousness becomes morbid or out of sorts, the body, though not always actually falling ill, loses in efficiency. Yet, let it be added, the body is less able to bear psychic illness than the inner self to bear physical illness. The body can never turn psychic suffering into nerve and muscle, but the psychic nature can weave malady into genius through the powerful operation of the Mystic Sense.

To be healthy is a commendable ambition. Being in good health, our desire is to become as immune as may be to disease, or being ill to give ourselves the best chance of recovery. Health is preserved by keeping body and mind in close relation to health-giving processes. It is not our concern to discuss in this connection questions of diet, sanitation, hygiene, exercise and similar aids to the promotion of health. Their value is of the first order and may not be ignored or discounted. But just now we are concerned with another part of human nature which has much to do in determining our condition of body—the sense which furnishes us with ideals.

The objective of an ideal is found in the idea flowing from the mind of God. It is as real to the Mystic Sense as a flower is to sight and smell. An ideal is the reflection of God's idea and is distorted or true according as the sense which perceives ideas is healthy or diseased. The Mystic Sense relates us to ideas, and enables us to touch, test, see and hear them, as truly as our bodily senses enable us to touch, test, see and hear the world of matter, form and sound. A healthy ideal is a vitalizing force, an unhealthy ideal is an invitation to disease. Ideals are subjectified ideas.

In the course of the development of that most experimental of all sciences, medicine, not only has dosing been reduced to a minimum, but also the natural recuperative powers of the patient have been discovered and are relied upon. The physician tries to open, for the sick, doors into nature's healthiest rooms. The patient being placed in a vitalizing environment is expected by the use of his will and Mystic Sense to respond to it. The physician alone can do but half the work. The will, and not only the willingness, to live, a mystical laying hold of the idea of health, is in all cases a valuable, in some an indispensable, factor in the process of recovery. The suggestion of health predisposes to health; the suggestion of disease is provocative of disease. Medicine may be both a material curative and a sacrament of health.

The habit of our day has been such as to create in us a marked pathological consciousness. The very process which, by slow degrees, has been driving disease to the wall, has produced in us a sensitiveness to the idea of disease that is inimical to health. The discovery of the causes of disease has peopled the imagination, even of those who have never looked through a microscope, with an army of hostile germs to the obscuration of those superior influences which conduce to well-being, until we have become chronically nervous of the hidden perils which beset our path. Insignificant pains are construed into the symptoms of the last disease discussed in the papers or the advertisement of a proprietary nostrum. Momentary fluctuations in health send us tripping with anxious brow to the doctor. Dabbling in pathology is an undesirable occupation, especially for the young. The wrappers of patent medicines, let alone the medicines themselves, have caused more agony than peace of mind and have been more provocative of disease than of health.

Happily we are emerging from the patent medicine stage.

A therapeutic consciousness ought to be the normal consciousness. The forces which make for life are in excess of those which make for death. The universe would go into steady decline were not the dominant forces salutary, and life would flicker out like the wick of a candle guttered in its socket. There is an inexhaustible fund of vitality open to man and we are competent to draw upon it so that we shall receive a maximum rather than a minimum. Part of the function of science is to put man into such a relation to the nature outside of him as to place the wholesome and remedial at his disposal, preventing disease by immunizing him from it. It is the common laws of health which are the most important. With the curious inconsistency which characterizes many human beings, we frequently see men adhering to some vigorous regimen of secondary or doubtful importance, while all the time they are flagrantly disobeying some primary law of health. The unity between the outer and the inner necessitates not only an intelligent and scientific treatment but also that which is mystical and more or less mysterious. Prayer, which is at once an appeal to the Source of Life to let loose saving health in our direction and an opening up of our being for the reception of hidden and unknown aid, is a higher form of psychic effort than either suggestion or auto-suggestion in that it includes both, though not precluding the concurrent use of either. Auto-suggestion looks only for self-induced benefit to the patient by application to an impersonal ideal; prayer does not think merely to apprehend a passive or indifferent remedy, but also to be apprehended by healthful, forceful Personality, like but superior to our own. A prayer to the ether would have in its reflex effect a totally different influence on the petitioner from a prayer to what was conceived to be a personal God. Similarly the quality of the virtue which is the result of mere ethical culture is as different from that which is the product of correspondence with the Christian's God as cotton is from linen. Nor is it that God is inactive until we pray. He is operating to the uttermost that our listless or passive or antagonistic personality will allow. The highest personality can do his best to the object of his love only when the latter adopts a responsive and co-operative attitude. The feeble spot in much, if not most, prayer, is that it asks without importunity, or importunes without appropriating. The Mystic Sense must reach up until it feels the hand containing the gift, and take the gift as its own. Auto-suggestion is a lame term indicating the application of the ideal to the defective. Suggestion is a similar application on the part of another to a companion. With a background of prayer, the insomnia patient can with profit watch the dream sheep go through the hedge, or lay himself in the cradle of old nursery rhymes, or welcome to his bedside the veiled legions of slumber as they troop forth on their silent errand from the presence of Him who giveth His beloved sleep.

Faith, which is simply the highest operation of the mystic sense, is as necessary to the complete work of healing as in the days when Jesus said, "According to thy faith be it unto thee." It appropriates to the full the remedial contents of scientific agencies which, under its touch become sacramental, and clothes the life in the soft robe of unanxious peace and serene cheerfulness. It is easy enough for a well man to talk to the sick concerning the desirability and curative value of a therapeutic consciousness. The depressed soul resents the necessity of being called upon to act independently of the body and in opposition to it. Most patients, too, for the time being are inclined to count each one his own case unique. But the Mystic Sense is wonderfully elastic. Cheerfulness comes by being cheerful, hope by being hopeful, calmness by being calm, healthymindedness by being healthyminded. This is the work of the Mystic Sense living in the realm of vigor even when the body is in distress. When the Mystic Sense goes exploring in high altitudes it never comes back empty handed. Even when it fails to return with health of body, it holds in its grasp health of mind. A blithe spirit in a feeble body can accomplish more than a sluggish spirit in a robust body. There are two kinds of healthymindedness— temperamental and acquired. The latter is the most powerful and may be had by anyone who cultivates his Mystic Sense.

The extent to which the Mystic Sense works toward a cure cannot be formulated. It varies with conditions. Of this we can be assured. It is always salutary, frequently indispensable. Diseases caused or induced by an abuse or morbid use of the imagination cannot be banished without the aid of the Mystic Sense as the chief agent. The imagination must be cured before the sickness can be cured, and there are instances when the cure of the imagination is the cure of the disease. That is none the less a disease, the seat of which is in the psychic, rather than in the physical part of self.

Two things remain to be said. First, our day is laying a dangerous accent on the value of mere physical life in man. It tends to foster physical self-consciousness and is an aspect of degrading materialism. All the efforts being put forth in the direction of making it possible for the physically feeble to survive, are dangerous, unless followed up by commensurate efforts to make them lit as characters. Mere existence and mere longevity are false gods.

It is haply justifiable for men of low breed, who honestly think this life the only one, to grasp at all its available gifts, and struggle to retain it on any terms for as long a period as may be. But not so among those who have risen to a knowledge of the meaning of immortality, even in its lesser aspects, of the perpetuation of the nation and the race, and the persistence of a man's work and influence among men after he himself has vanished. For such there is a higher food than mere life, beside which mere survival looks cheap and worthless.

> *"A man must live, we justify*
> *Low shift and trick to treason high,*
> *A little vote for a little gold*
> *To a whole senate bought and sold,*
> *By that self-evident reply.*
> *But is it so? Pray tell me why*
> *Life at such cost you have to buy?*
> *In what religion were you told*
> *A man must live?*
> *There are times when a man*
> *   must die,*
> *Imagine, for a battle-cry,*
> *From soldiers, with a sword to hold,*
>
> *   —*
>
> *From soldiers, with the flag*
> *   unrolled,—*
> *This coward's whine, this liar's lie,—*
> *A man must live!"*[1]

There is, however, a type of heroism which is not as uncommon as it seems to be for it is hidden —the type to which Kipling refers when he says:

> *"If you can force your heart and*
> *nerve and sinew*
> *To serve your turn long after they*
> *are gone,*
> *And so hold on, when there is*
> *nothing in you*
> *Except the will which says to them:*
> *'Hold on!'"*—

and once more we quote from another writer:

"Let us, for one thing, never forget that physical health is not the true end of human life, but only one of its most important means and conditions.... Death may and should be risked, the slow but certain undermining of the physical health may be laudably embarked on, if only the mind and character are not damaged, and if the end to be attained is found to be necessary or seriously helpful, and unattainable by other means."[2]

Secondly, special and mystical means of promoting or regaining health must have as a background the accumulated knowledge and scientific skill of the day. If there are individual exceptions here and there, they go to prove the rule. We can no more ignore the history of medical and chemical science, the findings of the microscope and laboratory, without disaster, than we can cut our country off from the traditions, laws and customs of yesterday without similar results. On the other hand, it is at least equal folly to flout or discredit the mystical experience of the ages. Human life, individually and corporately, is a unit, and due recognition must be given to all that goes to make it up.

---

1. Charlotte Perkins Stetson's In this our World.
2. The Mystical Element of Religion, vol. II, pp. 57, 58.

CHAPTER 3. IN RELATION TO THOUGHT

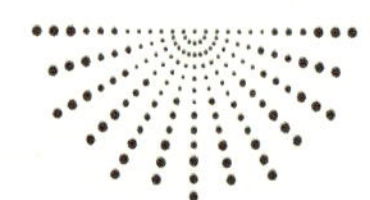

The mind includes the Mystic Sense in somewhat a similar way to the manner in which the body includes the physical senses. But the Mystic Sense can be, indeed must be, considered as a distinct faculty having a peculiar function in the formation of that product of the mind called thought, which is "the effort to win over facts to ideas, or to adjust ideas to facts."[1] The Mystic Sense can and does operate when the rationalizing faculty is reverently silent, and by its operation prepares new material for pure reason to consider.

There is no specifically intellectual organ. It is the whole man which apprehends knowledge just as it is the whole man and not an exclusively religious part of him, which apprehends and is apprehended by eternities and infinities. It is popularly supposed that science and mathematics call for the exercise of one set of faculties, and philosophy and religion another. Whereas the truth is that the same faculties are used for all alike in pretty much the same relation to one another. The Mystic Sense is as indispensable to science as it is to piety. Its method of operation is precisely the same in the one sphere as in the other.

We can best appreciate the important part the Mystic Sense plays in science by a survey of the foundations of accepted scientific fact. The whole body of our knowledge concerning the material universe is constructed upon a few ultimates, chief among them being the ether and the atom. The physical senses, so busy in that workshop of science, the laboratory, cease to be important when we deal with these fundamentals. The discoverer of ether never perceived it by touch, taste, smell, sight or hearing. Newton postulated it because he said it was a necessity, exactly as we postulate the existence of God. How could there be attraction across the measureless spaces which separate worlds if there were not some intangible substance? The ether was therefore discovered to order by the Mystic Sense and accepted because it proved a good working hypothesis. We are solemnly told by physicists that it is an "elastic solid," a "pervasive fluid," a "tenuous substance." And yet when we chase this elusive something into a corner we find it to be "that which undulates," a form of motion— well, so is a field mouse!

Again the atomic theory, first conceived by the Greeks, was restated by Dalton more than 2,000 years later, who brought it down "from the clouds to the laboratory and factory." But neither Dalton nor anyone else ever touched an atom, saw an atom, heard an atom, smelt an atom, or tasted an atom, ultimate of matter that it is. The physicist claims, however, "that though he cannot handle or see them, the atoms and molecules are as real as the ice-crystals in the cirrhus clouds that he cannot reach—as real as the unseen members of a meteoric swarm whose death glow is lost in the sunshine, or which sweep past us unentangled in the night"— that the atoms are in fact "not merely helps to puzzled mathematicians, but physical realities."[2] All this may be so. Nevertheless both the ether and the atom are so little material as to escape physical perception as completely as a ghost, and so nearly spiritual as to be perceived by the Mystic Sense with sufficient clearness to enable the scientist to use them as his fundamental hypothesis. If this reasoning be true, the ultimate of matter is spiritual and not material!

As with the ether so with the atom, it was a scientific necessity. The Mystic Sense contributed it to the laboratory, where it has been contentedly accepted as the ultimate of matter, until the other day, when someone opened the window of the atom to discover that it was a huge universe, of which a β corpuscle or electron was the least particle, related to the atom as a mote dancing in the sunbeam is to the room where it is. No sense but the Mystic Sense has yet sensed the electron. Not only, then, has science accepted the findings of the Mystic Sense, but, having accepted them, it has in the main not had reason to distrust them and continues confidently to base its research upon the foundation thus laid.

The freshest of more recent scientific discoveries, evolution, is as much the child of the Mystic Sense as of inductive reasoning. It was the Mystic Sense of ancient philosophers, exploring the unseen, which first descried it on the horizon as the sailor at the masthead spies the distant land. Darwin was the helmsman who steered the ship to port. He rationalized it and applied it as a working hypothesis. It is instructive to note that Darwin began his career with a rather acute sense of the mystical. He had a keen appetite for poetry, and pictures, and the music in King's College Chapel "gave him intense pleasure, so that his backbone would sometimes shiver."[3] He even began preparation for Holy Orders. In later life the interests that meant so much to him in youth died. "My mind," he says, "seems to have become a kind of machine for finding general laws out of large collections of facts, but why this should have caused the atrophy of that part of the brain alone, on which the higher tastes depend, I cannot conceive. A man with a mind more highly organized or better constituted than mine, would not, I suppose, have thus suffered; and if I had to live my life again, I would have made a rule to read some poetry and listen to some music at least once a week; for perhaps the parts of my brain now atrophied would thus have been kept active through use. The loss of these tastes is a loss of happiness, and may possibly be injurious to the intellect, and more probably to the moral character, by enfeebling the emotional part of our nature." It would be more accurate, perhaps, to explain this loss, not by atrophy but by too narrow specialization. His Mystic Sense and powerful imagination were not dead. They were centred on a single object. Having developed his Mystic Sense in one or all the ways open to him, a man may abandon its use in every direction but one. Christian worship, poetry, music prepare the Mystic Sense for that daring creation of hypotheses characteristic of Darwin. Without his power of hypothesis he could never have become more than a mere collector of the jackdaw order. He is his own best witness to the truth of this assertion. He says, "I have steadily endeavored to keep my mind free so as to give up any hypothesis, however much beloved (and I cannot resist forming one on every subject), as soon as facts are shown to be opposite to it," adding that he could not remember "a single first formed hypothesis which had not after a time to be given up or modified."

It is one of the chief functions of the Mystic Sense to present hypotheses. Without hypothesis the reason is a shorn Samson. A goal must be postulated, otherwise the wood could not be seen for the trees, and the intellect would be hopelessly lost in a tangle of underbrush and smothered by the weight of its own learning. "While theory is aimless and impotent without experimental check, experiment is dead without some theory passing beyond the limits of ascertained knowledge to control it. Here, as in all parts of natural knowledge, the immediate presumption is strongly in favor of the simplest hypothesis; the main support, the unfailing clue, of physical science is the principle that, nature being a rational cosmos, phenomena are related on the whole in the manner that conceptual reason would anticipate."[4] Generalization of a tentative character precedes and gives a starting point for induction. Hypothesis is more often the child of intuitive processes which capture thought by quick assault than of slower and more analyzable forces. First comes hypothesis, then the accumulation of data, finally, when all available evidence is in, rejection and the adoption of fresh hypothesis, or modification, or verification. "A bundle of disconnected facts is only the raw material for an investigation: their mere collection is the very earliest stage in the process; and even while collecting them there is nearly always some system, some place, some idea under trial."[5] The spiritual contents of the physical universe are, in part, evolution, the ether, the atom and such like. They bear material names, but they are ideas, out of reach of our sensory nerves, and capable of being perceived, first dimly and then clearly, only through the Mystic Sense. They form the allegorical department of scientific thought, and are to the reality as the Apocalypse is to the Kingdom of Heaven.

It would be without special gain, however easy, to multiply illustrations of the princely place which the Mystic Sense holds in scientific research. Let us, therefore, turn for a moment to mathematics with its array of imperturbable digits and prosaic facts. No sooner does the mathematician begin to move, than he finds it necessary to call to his aid the self-same faculty, which furnishes the physicist with his ether and atoms, and enables the worshipper to pray. Else how could he explore the fifth dimension, and define a line as having length without breadth, or a plane superficies as having only length and breadth, or a point as having no parts? It is not astonishing that the mathematician, "Lewis Carroll," was the author of those most delicious imaginative works of immortal fame, "Alice in Wonderland" and "Through the Looking-Glass." His vocation prepared and trained him for his avocation, and his avocation gave him new efficiency in his vocation. That which made him able to write the story of dreamland equipped him as an able scholar—the use in proper relation to his other mental gifts of the Mystic Sense. Similarly it is not surprising, but to be expected that Bacon, Pasteur, and Kelvin were, each in his own degree, religious men. They are the normal men of science, La Place, Huxley, and Haeckel being eccentrics and developed in a lop-sided way.

Invention, to turn to the department of practical science, relates the same story. Long before men saw, they dreamed. The locomotive was a vision before it was a fact; the aeroplane began as an idea, stinging men into adventurous experiment, before it spread its wings above the earth; men talked across vast spaces in thought before the earliest cable ticked its message, or the wireless system enthralled us by its wizardry. The Mystic Sense is prophetic and sees to-morrow as though it were to-day, dimly first and then with increasing clearness. "Without much dim apprehension, no dear perception; nothing is more certain than this."[6]

Still once more, when we turn to literature the Mystic Sense is a pole-star. History is a museum of the curios of yesterday, a pile of bones, a series of occurrences, a collection of bald facts as cold and bare as a heap of pebbles, until the Mystic Sense enters the sterile valley and brings with it the breath of life. An idiot with a memory can collect past facts as easily as a wee toddler can collect shells on the sea shore and to as good purpose. But it needs a man who, however vast his stock of information, possesses a developed Mystic Sense to classify facts and reveal their insides. Facts never tell the truth to an unimaginative mind. There is a higher form of accuracy and a deeper presentation of reality than a bare statement. Figures and prose, taken alone, are blind guides.

In normal childhood the Mystic Sense gets admirable training through the poetry and imaginative literature that belongs to the nursery in every nation. It is justly considered improper to confine a child's education to the multiplication table, scientific statement, religious dogma, and the memorizing of historic fact. The kindergarten, be its merits or defects what they may, is an endeavor to rouse the young mind to accurate observation and calculation through the imaginative faculty. Allegory, fable, and multiplied illustration form the natural vehicle for imparting knowledge to the young. The abstract is unintelligible, the bald is uninteresting; vivid description, poetical and highly colored, is the main road to knowledge. Care is taken to introduce fact in its best and prettiest clothing. Human life has a craving for the beautiful which is a phase of strength and an aspect of the real. Literature is the recorded expression of human life and thought, colored by the character of its various authors.[7] Art is literature on canvas, in vibrant sounds, and in stone.

Poetry is a necessary and not an ornamental part of literature. It is to a large extent the mystical embodiment of prose, or perhaps it would be truer to say that it bears somewhat the same relation to prose that hypothesis does to science. At any rate it is the distinctive literature of the Mystic Sense. It is the literature of the young nation just as much as it is of the young child. The earliest and the most permanent literature extant is either poetry or poetical in idea. Imagination, a child of the Mystic Sense, which runs wild unless disciplined, was born earlier than more sober offspring of the mind. Poetry is the parent of prose. The habit of the nursery or schoolroom is the reproduction on a small scale of the method of history—first poetry, then prose. He rules a nation who furnishes it with songs. There is no firmer foundation for national life than a great legendary epic or a garland of folk songs. The better, if not the larger, part of the Old Testament is poetic. Even the historical books do not pretend to be history as Gibbon and Green are history. Legend and history had not been distinguished from one another in those days. Legend is usually elaborately colored interpretation of fact where the actual occurrence has been lost in the interpretation, to such an extent that it can never be recovered or can only be guessed at. By subjective process, somewhat akin to reflection or digestion, the objective gains a new and transfigured self apart from and independent, it may be, of the original object. Thus legend is over-subjectified history. The outside is ignored for the sake of the inside.

Poetry and wholesome fiction must find permanent place in the life of a normal man. Do not delude yourself into thinking that your chief or only guides in life are logic and sense perception. They are not. Intuition and sentiment lead you twice for every once these others do. It is so much more comfortable, not to say honest and reasonable, to acknowledge frankly the primacy of your leaders, than to follow them and pretend all the while that you are following other guides, which is a species of disloyalty. Scientist, inventor, mathematician, man of letters, alike are not quite true to fact when they claim that pure reason and an exclusive process of induction control their mental operations. I would raise the question whether there is any such thing as the exclusively inductive method. Is it not truer to speak of the deductive-inductive than of the inductive? The Mystic Sense, with its adventurous and sometimes blundering progress, holds so important a place that without it logic and induction would be as grist without a mill. To reach knowledge by "pure reason" is as impossible as to reach the sun with a stepladder. Even supposing it were possible to bring bare reason over against bald fact, the result would reach only a degree beyond the achievement of a pig that counts, or a jackdaw that gathers a store of glittering objects.

I have heard scrupulous people complain of the effect of fairy lore, nursery fables, and imaginative traditions like that of Santa Claus, upon child life. It may be a question to consider, but it is dealing with a mote rather than with a beam. Cheap current literature, and the psychologically false story, which is characteristic of many of our magazines, are far more of an injury to heart and mind than the imaginative excesses of the nursery. The objection to the latter is not in the substance, but in the unnecessary attempts to deceive and to confuse objective and subjective in the child mind. Santa Claus is a harmless creature viewed as the Spirit of Christmas. When he is turned into a chimney god to whom written or spoken prayers are offered, it is another matter. Who can withstand the pathos of the little sister's death, resulting from her petition before the fireplace for a new toy for her baby brother? The flames took her and turned her into a burnt sacrifice to Santa Claus.

Supply is usually responsive to demand and the amount of imaginative literature and versifying in the journals of the day is a fair indication of the appetite for that which stimulates the Mystic Sense in letters. Also its hectic character is indicative of the wild state of the psychic life of the readers. The normal is counted uninteresting, and the abnormal, in incident and character, is portrayed. A steady diet of such reading leaves unhealthy blotches, indelible and disfiguring, on human life. Even in more serious literature the story of the abnormal may be given too great prominence. Valuable as the late Professor James's Varieties of Religious Experience may be, it has the fault of studying the abnormal as though it were the ordinary, leaving the great stretches of healthy religious experience practically untouched. If a physiologist were to give his main attention to men with one green and one brown eye, or with the heart on the right instead of the left side, or some kindred peculiarities, the sum total of his research would not contribute much to our knowledge of the normal man.

To conclude: every man who respects his mind, be his vocation what it may, has need to guard his Mystic Sense from defilement, and afford it opportunity for development. In what is technically known as education great stress is laid on proportion and subject matter. This is no less a necessity in maturer life than it is in youth. The same result ensues upon reading anything that comes to hand, that ensues upon eating anything that comes to hand. So important a thing is it, not only that we should be able to create hypotheses, but also that our hypotheses should be sound, that we must furnish our Mystic Sense with the same safeguards and stimulus that we afford our physical senses.

---

1. Royce's The World and the Individual, First Series, p. 58.
2. See Macfie's Science, Matter and Immortality, an admirable volume on this entire topic.
3. Darwin's Autobiography.
4. Sir Joseph Larmor in his Wilde Lecture (1908) quoted by Sir Oliver Lodge in Reason and Belief, p. 172.
5. Reason and Belief, p. 181.
6. The Mystical Element of Religion, vol. II, p. 265.
    The author quotes Kant—"we can be mediately conscious of an apprehension as to which we have no distinct consciousness." "The field of our obscure apprehensions, —that is, apprehensions and impressions of which we are

not directly conscious, although we can conclude without doubt that we have them—is immeasureable, whereas clear apprehensions constitute but a very few points within the complete extent of our mental life."

7. "Literature consists of those writings which interpret the meanings of nature and life in words of charm and power, touched with the personality of the author, in artistic forms of permanent interest."—Van Dyke's The Spirit of America, p. 242.

CHAPTER 4. IN RELATION TO CHARACTER

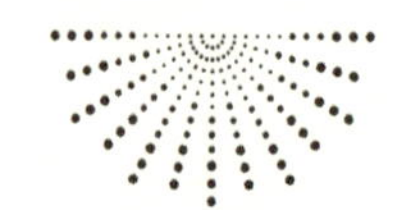

Good character is the reaction upon the whole self caused by the Mystic Sense as a habit visioning, and the will claiming, the excellent. It is the result on personality of a sustained effort to transcend the existing relation to life and its conditions, a state of chronic dissatisfaction with the progress and achievement of the moment, which makes the good mediocre by contrasting it with the superior and coveting the best conceivable as man's right and heritage.

The Mystic Sense is always finding a more excellent way. Excepting when taught to play casuistical tricks, it does not look for the conventionally proper, or rest comfortably in it.[1] It launches out into that noble freedom which, from a group of probabilities, selects that which is farthest removed from suspicion of selfish considerations and promises ultimately the best social results. On the other hand it is not disregardful of the accepted code of morals. This it takes as its foundation, individualizing it for personal use, and boldly submitting propositions for improvement to the social conscience for approval, modification, or rejection. Such approval, modification, or rejection is never a purely formal matter registered in the dictum of a tribunal but rather the culmination of a process akin, in the moral sphere, to that which is termed "natural selection" in the physical sphere.

Character and morality are not synonymous. Strong character may be good or bad, the latter being the result of the active exercise of the will in a conflict with goodness; it is the transformation of evil from a mere negation into a positive, personal force by conscious volition. But our study is of good character and its cultivation, so that when the word "character" is used the determinative "good" is understood.

Character is the result of the correspondence of personality with the best that it knows. It is measured by the faithfulness with which it responds to opportunity. A man with small opportunity, who is scrupulously conscientious in availing himself of all the privilege afforded him, becomes a stronger character than another, who, with his great opportunity, is less loyal in his use of it. Of course the greatest character is that which knows ideal virtue and consistently aims to bring up life to its level. Character is determined by reaction upon environment, external and internal. There are many suitable environments possible for every character, more than there are unsuitable ones, as the vicissitudes of most lives testify. Character is thus bound up closely with individual personality and is never abstract, as morality is in the science of ethics. Character is created and disclosed by that phase of experience in which the Mystic Sense is busied in photographing ideals on the film monopolized by the actual to the discomfiture and obliteration of the latter. Better to-morrows are obtruded on poor to-days, partly by virtue of the fact that the Mystic Sense is naturally in constant contact with the ideally best, sensing and appropriating it just as the body, without conscious effort on our part, senses and appropriates light and air, and partly because, either feebly or vigorously, most men claim for themselves by deliberate volition a larger life than that which is.

The possession of character is the sole justification of self-respect. Self-respect ensues upon the growth of character, and is to character what perfume is to the flower. It is due to the consciousness of having within ourselves that which is worthy— not mere moral acquiescence but something we have made peculiarly our own by active effort. It is a high form of the consciousness which inspires an inventor when he has constructed a piece of mechanism. Self-respect is a witness to our having been individualized and is indifferent to external possessions or aught that is our own by virtue of favor and chance rather than by merit. Self-respect runs into self-conceit and stagnation when it rests content with that which is. It never dawdles in its movements nor loafs on the street corners. Self-respect becomes self-contempt and self-abasement when our attention is turned from our cherished ideals and actual progress, and fixed upon our defects and failures. Penitence is not a bar but a necessity to character and its fragrant effluence, self-respect.

Character calls for and expects communal respect in the same degree that it receives self-respect. Reputation should be commensurate with character. It is possible for men to have the unmerited respect of their fellows without having self-respect. This is due to the practice of deceit, conscious or unconscious, which enables them to simulate character and have appearance without corresponding reality. To the man of character, it is as truly a pain to be overestimated as to be underestimated. He can afford to lose his reputation, though he can never be exempt from the keen pain involved. In the process of achieving character, the great frequently, if not always, have to endure the withholding of respect on the part of the community. Seldom does a man make a contribution to progress without being temporarily at least discredited by those whom most of all he is aiming to benefit. Self-respect towers at such moments. A man of character will trust himself when all men doubt him but make allowance for their doubting, too; he will wait and not be tired by waiting, or being lied about, won't deal in lies, or being hated won't give way to hating.[2]

Ideals become tasks and tasks become character in social experience. "A talent," says Goethe, "shapes itself in stillness, but a character in the tumult of the world." "That which would have remained only a quality in (our Lord), if He had stayed in the desert, becomes a life when He goes forth into the world." The ultimate test of a man's worth is his character and not his degree of morality —his power of volitional reaction upon environment, objective and subjective.

Every man at some time during his career,— most men for a considerable portion of it, and many from beginning to end,—covets character. Those who fail to claim it for themselves seldom fail to admire it in others. Frequently they put as much effort into pretending they have it as would win for them the real thing. They pay the price of gold for tinsel. Character has commercial value and sometimes men are honest according to law solely because it is politic, or polite according to social requirement because it pays. But the honesty and courtesy of such men are not virtues. They are handmaidens of covetousness. They contribute nothing to self-respect. They have no moral content, and serve only to aid in bolstering up a vicious characteristic. However, it is a tribute to the kingliness of character that, either for its market value or because of its inherent worth, men clothe themselves in its appearance when they do not seek the substance.

The substance may be had by every man. Man not only is, but also acknowledges himself to be, responsible for what he is. He makes the confession when he keeps his worst self from the public gaze even though it promises him no special gain. The extreme to which the sense of personal responsibility and accountability goes is evidenced by the fact that, though for others we find it difficult to believe in the closing of the possibility of self-improvement and ultimate loss fixed and final, many, perhaps most of us, think and act in our own case as though we at least shall be held strictly accountable for our character and reap as we live. If we had no responsibility for what we were and did, there would be no room for shame, were we to be publicly known to be exactly what we are. Rob Henley's poem of its defiant note and we are in the presence of sober fact:

"It matters not how strait the gate,

> *How charged with punishments the*
> *scroll—*
> *I am the Master of my fate—*
> *I am the Captain of my soul."*

Character, like fruit, gets rich flavor through living in a climate of extremes which give robustness by threatening very existence. The story of the transgression of Adam and his consort is illustrative rather than singular. The temptation set was the very stiffest to which human life, being what it is, could be subjected—a demand for self-discipline and obedience to mysterious law. It is interesting that the first recorded strain put upon the human will was not to do rather than to do. Seemingly it was the limitation of freedom, the restriction of choice, the narrowing of experience. In no other conditions could man have had a chance to gain character. Had our first human ancestors won their day without lapse, every succeeding generation would have had to do the same. You cannot inherit character. You must win it. Temptation is never eliminated from human life, as we know it. Its conquest in one form opens the door to its appearance in another form. Our earliest human ancestors having known the higher chose the lower. But this did not, either in their own case or in that of their offspring through a thousand generations, close the door to the attainment of character. Human life begins in conditions which threaten character and therefore becomes eligible for character. The complaint that there are those in the world who, because of hopeless environment, never have an opportunity, finds sympathetic echo in every heart, but it does not absolve us from responsibility to our own opportunity.

Much is made of heredity by those who know little or nothing of the controversies which gather about the study of its operation. The popular interpretation presses hard upon its thorns and forgets even the existence of its blossoms. "The sins of the fathers are visited upon the children unto the third and fourth generation," is the dominating thought which, by exclusive consideration, diseases the mind of many a man until his whole imaginative nature is employed in the service of some congenital, or supposed congenital, weakness to make him its victim. In this way fatalism is induced. Fatalism is a disease of the Mystic Sense which substitutes acquiescence for reaction. It is the straw committing itself to the river, not the oarsman using the current to his own advantage. Acquiescence is too tame a virtue for man, if indeed it be a virtue at all.

Whatever credit we give to heredity for endowing us with the tendencies of our evil forbears, we must give it equal credit for endowing us with those of our good forbears. If you are determined to be fatalistic, be so fairly, recognizing the possible transmission of every kind of tendency. Conscious acceptance of gifts of strength from the past is a powerful counter-irritant to defend us against a real or imagined inheritance of weakness.

The problem of heredity is obscured by the fog of controversy which just now envelopes it. We must remember that the main questions in doubt are its method, and extent, and our ability to intervene so as to modify or improve its operations. Science very cautiously says that "heredity suggests, though it would be rash to say it is proved, that man is almost entirely the product of inborn factors which are hardly affected by [physical] environment."[3] "Given parents of certain constitution, it can be said with confidence that on the average a certain proportion of their offspring will have such and such characters." "Both [the Biometrician and Mendelian] agree that what is present in the germ-cell will be present in the individual, and that external conditions as a rule play but a small part in determining its appearance." "Almost entirely," "hardly affected," "on the average," "a certain proportion," "as a rule," form a relatively large group of qualifying clauses in three short sentences. When we know more certainly the mechanism by which heredity operates we shall be better able by eugenics and physiological or mechanical processes to combat its evils and foster its benefits. In the meantime there is no call for us to stand idle. If man were mere animal it would be another matter, but he is not. His Mystic Sense, which links him to a superior order, has steadily differentiated him from all below him. It has enabled him to transcend environment. By means of it he can acquire character even if the laws of transmission should forbid him to pass it on to his offspring by congenital endowment. It is a finer and stronger thing to improve steadily the tradition of family or race by a series of successive personal conquests and achievements than to gain exemption from evil tendencies by the more or less mechanical process of procreation. Release from temptation is not necessarily a benefit, and is never as productive of character as the gift of ability to defeat it. Frequently all that is needed is inspiration, mystical and human, to enable a man to rise above his evil inheritance and habit. Evil tradition is as real and destructive a phase of heredity as inborn weakness, whereas on the other hand noblesse oblige. It is rather the tradition of the family trait of intemperance than a transmitted physical peculiarity that keeps the line of drunkards unbroken. Children must not be allowed to suppose that they can be excused from struggle. Being prepared for all temptations as a normal part of experience they are least likely to become victims of any: being made expectant of all virtues, they may perchance glean some.

Our environment is our opportunity, particularly in those spots where it is uncongenial and threatening. To chafe and fret is to increase the inimical possibilities of difficulty. To think of it except with the intention of mastering it is weakening and depressing. To remove it with our own hands rather than have another remove it, if it be moveable, or, should it be immoveable, to weave it as material into our scheme of life, using its rough threads to the last stand, is to achieve character. A man must either fit his burden to his back or his back to his burden, if he desires to remain man. They are rare exceptions in mankind who have not capacity for so doing, if not by themselves, at any rate in a sympathetic social setting. A burdened life by the free use of the Mystic Sense may become a privileged life. Introduce fearlessness and experimental curiosity into hardship, and you get romance which keeps the wings of life moving and mounting, and makes the world of men around look up in aspiring wonder.

> *"There is no storme but this*
> *Of your owne Cowardise*
> *That braves you out;*
> *You are the storme that mocks*
> *Your selves; you are the rocks*
> *Of your owne doubt:*
> *Besides this feare of danger, ther's*
> *no danger here;*
> *And he that here feares danger, does*
> *deserve his feare."*[4]

The Mystic Sense has an inner ear. Through it conscience delivers its message by means of which we come to know and understand the meaning of ought and ought not. Ready response to conscience is to be coveted above all things, especially where conscience has been trained and illumined. A friend once wrote me, a few days before his death, that he had come to see that what pretended to be education was no education at all unless it included the development of conscience. But mere knowledge of right and wrong, ought and ought not, does not impart goodness. To be aware that vice injures and virtue blesses is desirable but insufficient. There is not less vice among those who know than there is among those who do not know ethics, other things being equal, excepting where education is conceived to be something more than the imparting of information.

Sometimes nations and individuals covet character without being ready to pay the whole price for it. They give admirable facilities for the development of certain phases of training essential to character, but exclude that deciding factor which determines whether or not they may be woven into character. Influences from other sources may come in to repair wilful neglect, but, if not, the training goes for nothing so far as character is concerned. Public schools can never give character its best opportunity without a practical recognition of religion. Purely secular education, the imparting of learning including the science of ethics, without religion in church and home to supplement it, is a doubtful blessing at best. The current idea of secular education is not new. During the French Revolution its leaders mapped out what appeared to be a satisfactory programme of instruction. It was desired to have moral training, first without religion or with the "Worship of Reason," then with a minimum of religion. The priests were suffered to continue as being at any rate moral policemen, but Danton planned to supplant them by officiers de morale. All experiments were of no avail. "La morale populaire ... cherche encore," it was pathetically complained, "un point d'appui solide." Then came freedom to worship, and later the Concordat reintroduced the old religious order, partially, it is true, because the people could or would not live without it, but largely for the sake of morals.

If religion without morality becomes superstitious sentiment, morality without religion becomes for the average man inoperative ethics and ultimately a pitiless judge. There is no more oppressive tyrant than a high ethical code with a will, untrained, uninspired, and helpless to respond. It becomes a mocking and cruel Nemesis viewing with indifference its writhing victims. The Chinese Classics are preserved by the wonderful nation who produced them, as a literary treasure instead of as a practical code of conduct—the sure fate of the Bible apart from the Christian Church.

It is too late in the day to pretend that morality and religion are synonymous, however intimate their relationship, or that the end of religion is to make men good. Righteousness, which is the Christian term for morality, is to be had only in part by the practice of embracing the excellent and bathing our mystic self in the fountain of ideals. The type of righteousness thus created can never be aught than self-conscious, like an overdressed woman, or a gaudy painting. The Mystic Sense must occupy itself in still higher altitudes. Having come from God and being partaker of His nature, it must aspire to Him. The end of life is religion, and the end of religion is to know God. The purest type of righteousness, experienced or conceivable, is created by our having as our dominant ambition to know the only God and Jesus Christ whom He hath sent. The net result is Christian Character.

---

1. "The wealthy class in Rome and all over Italy began to conform to that conventional code of propriety by which the rich seem always destined, in the progress of civilization, to become more and more enslaved, till finally they lost all feeling for what is serious and genuine in life. The new generation followed their example with alacrity, and preached the new conventions with a passionate vehemence which must have been highly exasperating to those of their seniors who were still attached to the simplicity of primitive manners. Amongst those who protested against this development there was, however, one prominent figure of the younger age, Marcus Porcius Cato, a man of rich and noble family, and a descendant of Cato the Censor. His puritan spirit revolted against the tyranny of fashion to which the golden youth of Rome wished to make him conform; he would walk in the streets without shoes or tunic, to accustom himself, as he

said, only to blush at things which were shameful in themselves, and not merely by convention."—Ferrero's Greatness and Decline of Rome, vol. I, pp. 135, 136.
2. Kipling's If—.
3. Doncaster's Heredity in the Light of Recent Research (1910), p. 113 ff.
4. Crashaw.

CHAPTER 5. IN RELATION TO RELIGION

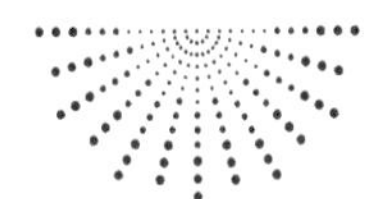

The operation of the Mystic Sense in relation to religion is commonly called faith. Conversely, faith under another name is that operation of the Mystic Sense which promotes health of body, which affords a starting point for all intellectual, scientific, and other productive pursuits, which leads character from strength to strength. The subjective conditions under which, and the spheres in which, the Mystic Sense is employed, differ. But the faculty itself and its modus operandi are always the same. Just as the sense of bodily sight which views the dirt beneath our feet is the same sense which contemplates the blue sky, so the inner sense of sight which perceives an electron, an ideal, or a hypothesis is the same sense which sees God. It is as possible to see God as to see a hypothesis, and as possible (not more and probably less), to see a hypothesis as to see God.[1]

It is fitting that the most exalted operation of the Mystic Sense should be dignified by a distinctive term, provided that in so doing no room is given for the implication that there is a faculty, or set of faculties, used in religion alone. A man has religious capacity because he is man, and not because he is a specially favored individual of his kind. Man, unless he abdicates his manhood, a task so difficult as to verge on the impossible, must live by his Mystic Sense; he must keep touch with the unseen, or cease to be a man. To be a man, rounded and proportioned, complete and splendid, he must use his Mystic Sense not merely here and there but everywhere. The Mystic Sense has as true an existence in the whole personality, and relation to it, as the physical sense of touch, and is as acutely sensitive to the stimulus of the spiritual phase of reality as the body is to that of the material. It is analogous to all the sub-divisions of the nervous system but chiefly to sight and hearing, the most distinguished of the senses.[2]

To perceive an ideal is as real a sensation as to look at a flower. An impression is left behind not unlike the photograph of the flower retained on the retina of the eye and revived by act of memory and will. But the visualizing has nothing to do with physical sense perception, and the part of the personality thus impressed is spiritual. To characterize tactual sensation of the body as real necessitates a like characterization of the tactual sensation of the spirit. If it be argued that in the latter relationship there is no certainty as to what is phantasm and what reality, let it be remembered that the history of science is largely a series of corrections of imperfect sense records. A highly developed power of observation with ability for accurate registration and correlation is the distinguishing feature of culture. The Mystic Sense, like the bodily senses, is capable of increasingly accurate perception by skilful and disciplined use. It takes its beginnings in gropings like the awkward jerks of a baby's limbs, and develops into ordered and reliable movement by exercise and experiment, which includes mistakes and the profit accruing to the experience. Superstition bears the same relation to faith that a false scientific hypothesis bears to ascertained fact. The Mystic Sense in its infant working catches a distorted view of the ideal, as when Darwin propounded his conception of heredity by pangenesis, and leads us astray in science; in like manner in religion a glimpse, through a mist of ignorance and moral deficiency, of the Absolute, eventuates in superstition. Both are necessary stages in the training of the Mystic Sense. Similarly to the way in which the theory of pangenesis stimulated discussion and research so as to aid the Mystic Sense to a more accurate perception of the true hypothesis of the manner of heredity, the superstitions of the nations conceived in sincerity, crude and even repulsive though they be, have contributed to the complete knowledge of God and His character which forms our most valuable heritage.

It is not hazardous to say that the ideals and hypotheses which are still waiting for the cognition of the Mystic Sense transcend gloriously those thus far apprehended. This means that science is in its infancy. It is equally true to assert that religion, so far from having fallen into decline, is but girding itself to scale heights impatient to feel the tread of human feet. That which is good and true in itself must persist, whatever its crudeness and blemishes. The Mystic Sense in relation to religion is only at the beginning of its history. Human, that is mystic, life began at so remote a period as to be beyond the reach of research. The operation of the Mystic Sense through many thousands of years[3] prior to human records led the way to that ordered approach to God which we call religion. The possibilities of its growth for the race at large are indicated and emphasized by individual instances taken from the common crowd. The world is just at this moment engrossed in seeing that every one should have an opportunity of developing fine physique and of acquiring information. It is assumed that under proper conditions a high average may be reached. The same is to be postulated for the development of the Mystic Sense in relation to the highest and best in religion. Under a sufficient stimulus the average man will be able to apprehend what now is reached only by a minority. This, however, can not come to pass until a whole world of men strain their inner eye and quicken their inner ear in the same direction, each contributing of his own strength to the rest, and all to each.

The history of Christianity and its immediate progenitor, Judaism, is the record of the highest development of the Mystic Sense in religion. In the course of its progress the Absolute rises from a dim shadow to the greatest Reality. It is distinctively the religion of orderly and rational mysticism. At first, men, feeling the working of the Mystic Sense, used it in a childish way. What was splendid in them would be culpable in us. Abraham could consider it a call of God to slay his son: a man of to-day could only think of it as a monstrous crime against God and society, revolting even to contemplate. It marked a stage in the rationalizing of faith when at the last moment Abraham saw mystically that it was not God's purpose that any human being should ever do at His bidding an inhuman deed.

The most perfect individual life of faith ever lived was that of Jesus Christ. His Mystic Sense never erred. He was never so exclusively Divine as not to be completely human. He was God living the life of man. He walked by faith, not by sight. Visions and ecstasies found rare and momentary place in His experience. He reached His goal by the use of those gifts and endowments which we have in common with Him, and proclaimed forever to the race of men that it is the simple, steady, patient exercise of the Mystic Sense toward a God who is revealed as Love, which exalts human life and puts it in the way of winning incomparable power and beauty. His reply to the query, What shall we do, that we might work the works of God, is, This is the work of God, that ye believe—believe on Him whom He hath sent. Further, He makes the astounding prophecy, Assuredly I announce that he that believeth on me, the works that I do shall he do also; and greater works than these shall he do. The early Christians were distinguished from their fellows as men who exhibited in high degree the faculty of belief so as to be in a unique sense "Believers," and their religion was one in which faith played so prominent a part as to merit the name of "The Faith." The whole Christian era has been an era of faith or the exercise of the Mystic Sense. No great work can be found in it, in science, literature or religion which has not been made possible by the stimulus given to faith by the influence of Jesus. Miracles do not cease to be miraculous when they cease to be mysterious, and the Christian centuries are strewn with such miracles—many of them, works of healing and moral restoration, as great as those of Jesus. But the greater works than His still lie before us when we have sufficiently shed materialism and committed ourselves more implicitly to the life of faith.[4]

The disappearance into the spirit world of Jesus has made that world human,[5] so that the Mystic Sense can be as truly at home in it as it is in scientific research. He prepared for His withdrawal thither by centring the attention of His friends upon it. His manifestations after His death on the cross were primarily to the Mystic Sense of His followers. That is to say, those unaccustomed to use the Mystic Sense in a religious way were incapable of seeing Him. It was impossible for Him to show Himself to the irreligious or enemies of God. This does not mean that it was only to the Mystic Sense of believers that He manifested Himself, but also to their bodily senses by way of the Mystic Sense. There is much that comes to the cognizance of the Mystic Sense through physical perception, and unless there is a refined and cultured nervous organism there is no mystical connotation. A Peter Bell could not find the mystical in nature.

> *"A primrose by a river's brim*
> *A yellow primrose was to him,*
> *And it was nothing more."*

The same primrose to a Linnæus or an Asa Gray would reveal an unseen world. Conversely, there are some things which cannot affect our physical being except by the way of mystical experience. Striking instances of this sort have been suitably termed by von Hügel "psycho-physical."

They are possible only where there is extraordinary sympathy between the mystical and physical, the latter having been made very completely the servant of the former. Only the mystic, or the specialist in the use of the Mystic Sense, is eligible for such experiences. The tremendously real fellowship with the Risen Lord of the disciples was of an ecstatic or psycho-physical order. It degrades the Resurrection manifestations to overemphasize their physical reality as though this, rather than the mystical, were the important feature. Their dominant note is spiritual. The physical perception came through the mystical. The experience of the disciples could not be reproduced in after times with other men, for the necessary conditions were wanting. Here and there among spiritual giants there is a well authenticated psycho-physical experience, but it is of phenomenal rather than of spiritual or moral value. And yet it is within our power to see the Christ as really and effectively as the Apostles did, though not wholly after the same manner.

St. Paul did not begin his life of faith when he had his psycho-physical experience on the road to Damascus. He reached there a turning point in its history. He was converted, turning his mystic powers in a new direction. Those who were with him were not sufficiently developed to see all that he saw or hear all that he heard.[6] His vision of Jesus was momentary but his life of faith was continuous. If faith was at its beginning when Abraham made his venture, it reached an illustrative and inviting climax when St. Paul made his. It was greater for St. Paul to espouse the cause of the Christ than to have a vision of Jesus. The phenomenal or extraordinary does not always culminate in such courage and devotion as his. It was because he was a mystic that he had his vision, not because he had a vision that he became a mystic. The Apostles who knew Jesus in the flesh had a lesser opportunity for faith than St. Paul who saw Him but once and then after psycho-physical fashion, and who never apprehended Him with all his bodily senses like those who saw "with their eyes" and "beheld," and whose "hands handled" the Word of Life. It was fitting that St. Paul should give Christianity the impetus which made it a world religion. The highest development of faith has assigned to it the biggest undertaking. St. Peter with undeveloped intellectual gifts and faith based on sight could not do what St. Paul with highly developed reason and singular faith could do. The Risen Jesus Himself declared that faith dependent upon physical or psycho-physical experience is of a lower order than that in which the mystic sense is independent of phenomenal action of the bodily sense—Because thou hast seen me, thou hast believed: blessed are they that have not seen, and yet have believed.

The great multitude of mortals will always be outside of psycho-physical experiences. There is no religious loss in the fact. Rather the contrary.

That which gives the soul its permanent hold upon moral and spiritual realities and regard for them in mystics is not their rare psycho-physical experiences, but the same exercise of the Mystic Sense in the daily round of commonplace religious duty which is open to every human being, with like wonderful results upon character. A phenomenal spiritual occurrence in the case of one who was not living a religious life would be a mere wonder, perhaps even productive of spiritual harm.[7] Such experiences are never to be sought for. If they come their peril is not less than their inspiration.

> *"The trivial round, the common task,*
> *Will furnish all we need to ask,*
> *Room to deny ourselves, a road*
> *To bring us daily nearer God."*

It is a great barrier to religious effort among the crowd, for those living the life of faith, to give the impression that their experience is one of a series of ecstasies. It is no more so than is that of a student of science or higher mathematics. It is the life of faith open to all men which forms the religious life of the best men and the best religious life of all men—the constant placing of God before the Mystic Sense in a way not dissimilar from that in which the scientist approaches his hypothesis.

*"Think not the Faith by which the
  just shall live
Is a dead creed, a map correct of
  heaven,
Far less a feeling fond and fugitive,
A thoughtless gift, withdrawn as
  soon as given;
It is an affirmation and an act
That bids eternal truth be present
  fact."*

Though the Mystic Sense is not the sole religious faculty, it holds the primacy here as in every distinctively human activity. Used with reason its operation becomes reasonable or rational faith. Its opposite is not reason but sight, that is to say, the unaided findings of the bodily senses of which sight, being the most princely, is representative. Hence St. Paul's contrast—we walk by faith, not by sight. Even here it is hardly fair to say there is antagonism. Sight is the enemy of faith only when it refuses to be an ally. Sight sees, faith in-sees and therefore fore-sees. Sight has boundaries which it cannot pass. Faith has horizons which retreat as it advances.

Faith has become increasingly rational as the world has grown older and experience has been added to experience. Its explorations in the world of ideals have been more frequent and daring with the advance of time. Consequently the man of to-day makes his flights thitherwards with a fulness of assurance on rational grounds or grounds of high probability which would have been impossible to an Abraham. If the triumphs open to faith have multiplied, so have the deterrent forces holding it back or set in battle array to thwart or otherwise impair it. The commonest injury wrought upon faith is the deflecting of it from the worthy to the unworthy or less worthy. If a man's Mystic Sense, acute in other directions, is dormant or sluggish in religion, the reason is usually to be found, I think, in circumstances analogous to those which make a student of belles lettres, for instance, indifferent to science, or a philosopher careless of the exploits of commerce, cases of which are not wanting. The mind finds higher pleasure among certain persons in being exclusive and technical than in being catholic. So the Mystic Sense can fall short of its highest employment simply because there is not in its possessor the will to employ it commensurately with its capacity. The explanation why some men are not actively religious must be sought elsewhere than in the contention that they are short a faculty. The Mystic Sense, which by virtue of their humanity they possess, is not employed by them religiously from whatever reason—defective interest, prejudice, antagonism, environment. Nevertheless the same inner sense is pushed to its fullest activity in other directions. The faculty which by a daring leap fixes on the evolutionary hypothesis, or with imaginative subtlety suggests the plot of a novel, is the self-same one which enables us to say, "Our Father, which art in heaven." The consideration of vicious men who are irreligious does not come within the purview of this discussion. Religion and vice are mutually exclusive, though piety and immorality are not, so that we have the anomaly of immoral character revelling in pious practices.

One thing remains to be said. The use of the Mystic Sense in religion, more perhaps than in any other sphere, cannot begin and end in individualism. It is requisite for each to submit the results of his mystic excursions and explorations to the conclusions of the most advanced religion. Mystic observation and experience must have the support and purification of universal mystic experience that will distinguish between the false and the true, phantasm and reality, and deliver the individual from eccentricity and extravagance. In other words, a church is more necessary than a chamber of commerce, a national government, or an academy of science. Mystic experience must be organized like all other experience. As the world grows older and man wiser, organization develops and broadens. National societies and alliances become international and a parliament of man seems a reasonable goal toward which to press. Human life in its individual aspect finds its fullest freedom in organization and not apart from it. The idea of the Catholic Church is as old as Christianity. One Body, one spirit, one

Lord, one Faith, one Baptism, said St. Paul before Christianity was fifty years old—and the use of the Mystic Sense independently of organized Christian experience cannot hope to reach valuable results. Reformers of religion are eccentrics and detract from their service so far as they ignore the religious experience of the ages by assuming exclusive positions or lifting a doctrine out of its setting. Our Lord never broke with the faith of His fathers. His last act was to partake of the Passover according to the law. It was the Jews who broke with Him. He came not to destroy but to fulfill. The only setting for any one part of the truth is all the rest of the truth. The only relationship big enough for any one man is all the rest of mankind. When at last the disturbed and broken Christian Church comes to rest in the large scheme of unity planned by its Founder, then the mystical life of man will gain a power and splendor which now is but a vision and a hope.

This concludes my endeavor to credit the Mystic Sense with that dignity and position of importance which belongs to it by right. The attempt is crude and the brilliant vision which I had at the beginning of my task has become dimmer under the process of putting it into words. Whatever has been written stands as a contribution of thought and experience which cannot be of much value until it has been purified from the dross of individualism through the findings of religion and science, and lost in the great volume of truth to which I submit it with reverence and loyalty.

---

1. A hypothesis receives passively our quest: God moves to meet us.
2. Newman in his Dream of Gerontius endows the disembodied soul with perceptive powers analogous to those of the body, saying only the sense of sight. Thus:

> Soul. "I cannot of thy music rightly say
> Whether I hear, or touch, or taste the tones."
> ... "How comes it then
> That I am hearing still, and taste, and touch,
> Yet not a glimmer of that princely sense
> Which binds ideas in one, and makes them live?"
> Angel. "Nor touch nor taste, nor hearing hast thou now;
> Thou livest in a world of signs and types,
> The presentation of most holy truths,
> Living and strong, which now encompass thee.
> A disembodied soul, thou hast by right
> No converse with aught beside thyself;
> But, lest so stern a solitude should load
> And break thy being, in mercy are vouchsafed
> Some lower measures of perception,
> Which seem to thee, as though through channels brought,
> Through ear, or nerves, or palate, which are gone.
> ...
> How, even now, the consummated Saints
> See God in heaven, I may not explicate;
> Meanwhile, let it suffice thee to possess
> Such means of converse as are granted thee,
> Though, till that Beatific Vision, thou art blind."

The idea underlying the Beatific Vision is the complete apprehension of God by the complete man. Sight is chosen to denote this bliss because it is a princely co-ordinating sense, and our Lord spoke of the heritage of the pure in heart as being the vision of God, a heritage let it be noted, however, for now and not merely for hereafter. It seems reasonable to suppose that our powers of perception after death will be those mystic powers which we enjoy and use now, though then they will be rapidly developed as being our only perceptive powers.

This suggests the investigation in progress of psychic phenomena by scientific methods. The result may lead to an increase of our knowledge regarding the nature of such phenomena. But I do not see how, if communication with the departed be possible at all, we can expect to reach, and be reached by, them except through the Mystic Sense. The invocation of Saints seems to me more in line with what is probable than some of the experiments of the day. Disembodied spirits presumably approximate the nature of God and can approach or be approached only after a purely spiritual or mystical fashion, excepting in those rare psycho-physical instances which are themselves contingent upon a highly developed mystical character and experience.

3. Progressive civilization may be said to have begun 8,000 b. c.
4. Two things must be remembered in connection with the interpretation of Jno. XIV ff. In the first place, these chapters, bursting as they are with startling promises which the critic claims have not been made good, were addressed to a select and specially trained group of followers. For instance, Whatsoever ye shall ask in my name, that will I do, constitutes a promise that could not have been made to a heterogeneous crowd. It presupposes an understanding of the mind of Christ that keeps prayer within its appointed limits. A promise of this sort made to a St. John would be fulfilled, whereas it could not be fulfilled in the case of a man who thought that a prayer for the success of his lottery ticket, or the triumph of a competitive business scheme stained with dishonor, might be offered in the name of Jesus. In the second place, these chapters were written down and became accepted Scripture not less than three quarters of a century after they were spoken, by one who, in common with like-minded companions, had experienced the faithfulness of our Lord's promises. These men knew them to be true, not merely because our Lord had said them, but also because Christian experience, had verified

them. This is so of the entire Gospel record. That was remembered and recorded which Christian experience had verified.

5. Similarly His advent into our human world made it Divine.
6. Acts IX, 7; XXII, 9.
7. The miracles of Moses before Pharaoh are illustrative of that which abounds in history—wonders hardening further an irreligious life.

~

9 782357 285057